It's me... a Pig

Om
KIDZ
An imprint of Om Books International

First Published in 2019 by

Om KIDZ | Om **Books International**

Corporate & Editorial Office
A-12, Sector 64, Noida 201 301
Uttar Pradesh, India
Phone: +91 120 477 4100
Email: editorial@ombooks.com
Website: www.ombooksinternational.com

© Om Books International 2019

ISBN: 978-93-86410-50-4

Printed in India

10 9 8 7 6 5 4 3 2 1

Sales Office
107, Ansari Road, Darya Ganj
New Delhi 110 002, India
Phone: +91 11 4000 9000
Email: sales@ombooks.com
Website: www.ombooks.com

Contents

WHO ARE YOU?

Hello! I am a pig.

I am a mammal who belongs to the Suidae family.

Scientific Name

Sus scrofa domesticus

of the Domestic Pig

Litter Size

Pigs can give birth to 7 to 12 piglets at a time.

We have a **stout** body and short legs. We have thick skin that is usually coated with stiff hair.

Leathery Snout

Pigs use their snouts to search for food. They rely heavily on their great sense of smell because they have poor eyesight.

A new word to learn

Stout - fat or heavy build

WHAT DO YOU EAT?

Taste buds

While humans have 10,000 taste buds, pigs are known to have 15,000 taste buds!

We are omnivores which means that we eat both plants and animals. Wild pigs eat grass, plants, fruit, wild flowers, and so on. Domesticated pigs are mostly fed corn and soyabean meals.

WHERE DO YOU LIVE?

We live in grasslands. When in the wild, we are usually found in moist forests, swamps and shrublands.

Sty

A sty or pigsty is the name given to an enclosure where domestic pigs are raised.

Enclosure - area surrounded by a barrier

A new word to learn

HOW DO YOU COMMUNICATE?

We oink, squeal and grunt to communicate with each other. We have over 20 different vocalisations.

Noisy Squeals

A pig's squeal can be as loud as 100 decibels, higher than the sound of a supersonic aeroplane!

HOW BIG ARE YOU?

We usually weigh between 140 and 300 kg. Domestic pigs are raised to be heavier. Wild pigs are known to grow up to 7 ft in length.

Good Swimmers

Pigs are known to be excellent swimmers over short distances.

WHAT ARE YOUR BABIES CALLED?

Our babies are called piglets. A group of piglets is called a farrow.

Baby Pigs

Baby pigs have several names such as piglets, shoats, weaners and feeders.

Voice Recognition

Piglets can recognise their mother's voice. Also domestic piglets learn to respond to their names by the time they are 2 weeks old.

We have an average lifespan of about 15 to 20 years. Wild pigs, on the other hand, may live up to 20 years.

DO YOU SWEAT?

No. We cannot sweat. So when it's hot we pant and roll in the mud to stay cool.

Clean Animals
Pigs are actually very clean animals and if they are given enough space, they never dirty the areas where they sleep or eat.

Yes. Our skin is tough but it is extremely sensitive to temperature and injury.

Protection from Sunlight

Pigs love rolling in the mud. Mud helps to protect their sensitive skin from sunburn.

CAN YOU RUN?

Yes. We can run at a speed of about 11 miles per hour. We may look clumsy but we are very strong and **swift** animals.

A new word to learn

Swift - quickly

Walk Time

Pigs have four toes on each foot but they use only two of them to walk.

Boars and Sows

A male pig is known as a boar. A female pig is known as a sow.

There are several species of pigs in the world. We prefer to live in close-knit groups known as sounders. A sounder consists of one boar and several sows and their babies.

WHAT IS YOUR NOSE CALLED?

My nose is called a snout. I use my snout to smell, find food and dig holes.

Strong Sense of Smell

Pigs have an excellent sense of smell. It is so well developed that they can easily find things underground using their snout.

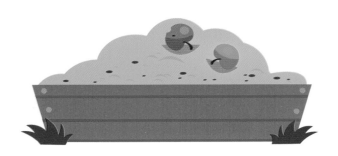

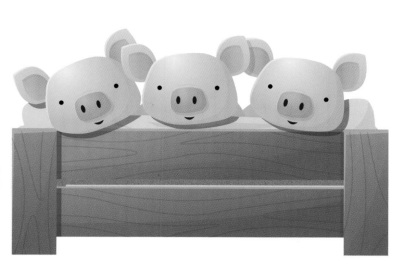

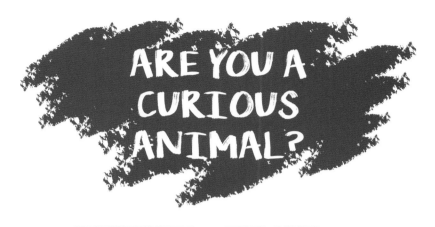

ARE YOU A CURIOUS ANIMAL?

Amazing Pets

It is said that pigs are easier to train than dogs or cats. Pigs can be trained to walk with a leash around their neck, use a litter box and even perform tricks.

Yes. We are curious and **insightful** creatures who are known to be smarter than 3-year-old children, dogs and even some primates.

A new word to learn

Insightful - showing a deep understanding

DO YOU HAVE TEETH?

Yes. An adult pig has 44 teeth. The canine teeth called tusks grow continuously and are very sharp.

Tusks

Milk Teeth

Piglets have 28 milk teeth that fall out and are replaced by a set of 44 permanent teeth.

Where's the Sky?

Pigs have a vast field of vision, but they can't look up at the sky when they are standing. This is because it is very difficult for them to bend their neck backwards.

We have very poor eyesight and our ability to focus on things, visually, is weak.

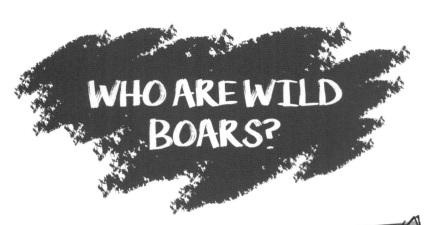

The wild boar is a species of the wild pig. It is also known as the European wild boar. Wild boars are the largest wild pigs and are found in several regions across the world.

A new word to learn

Provoke - deliberately make someone angry

Tusks

Wild boars have sharp tusks. Even though they are not aggressive animals, they can be dangerous when **provoked**.

The Bornean bearded pig is a species of pig found mostly in Sumatra, Borneo and the Malay Peninsula. They have yellowish whiskers on their faces and on the bridge of their noses.

A new word to learn

Whiskers - long projecting hair growing from the face or snout of many mammals

Social Animals

Bearded pigs are intelligent and social animals. They live in small groups.

ACTIVITY TIME

FOAM PAPER PIG

Things You'll Need

- Pink foam paper
- Marker
- Scissors
- Glue bottle
- Googly eyes

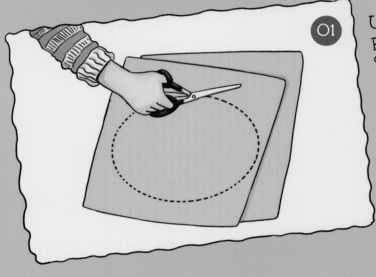

Using pink foam paper, draw and cut out the different parts of the pig's body.

These are all the parts required to make your foam paper pig.

03

Now paste the head and legs of the pig to its body.

04

Now add the pig's ears, snout and mouth.

05

Finally, paste the googly eyes on the pig's face, and add a curly tail.

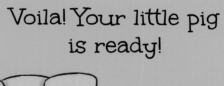

Voila! Your little pig is ready!

Help the mommy pig reach her piglets!